Telling Australia's Truth

Telling Australia's Truth

Poems selected by Stephen Matthews

Telling Australia's Truth
ISBN 978 1 76109 695 2
Copyright © text individual authors 2024
Copyright © this collection Ginninderra Press 2024
Cover image: Ginninderra Press

First published 2024 by
Ginninderra Press
PO Box 3461 Port Adelaide 5015
www.ginninderrapress.com.au

Contents

Introduction	Stephen Matthews	9
Perhaps, After All, There is Hope	John Watson	11
Utopia	Christopher Palmer	12
Dante's Lane	Mary Chydiriotis	13
Recipe for a Democracy Sausage	Anne Morgan	14
Lurch On	Linda Wells	15
The Response, 14 October 2023	Rosanna E. Licari	16
The Day the Voice Went Silent	Jonathan Shaw	17
Sorry, no change	Kavita Nandan	18
White speaks to black	Elizabeth Heij	19
An end of kindness?	Geoffrey Lilburne	20
Coloured by Disparity	M. Fermanis-Winward	21
Where can we go after 'No'?	Helen Seymour	22
It Takes Time To Know	Maurice Whelan	23
Summertime in Australia	Mandy Toczek McPeake	24
Can we be one and free?	Writing from the Heart	25
Colony	Karen Throssell	26
From the Heart of a Rock	Satendra Nandan	27
Post referendum observation	Valerie Volk	28
no Voice as yet	Ray Tyndale	29
Uluru Games of the Heart	Janet Upcher	30
The Forgotten Voices of Australia	Deborah Anne Tanzer	31
The vote	Greg Tome	32
'Straya, no worries	John Bartlett	33
Australia's Referendum on the Voice	Thérèse Corfiatis	34
referendum	Dawn Bruce	35
Terra Nullius	Liz Newton	36
Voiceless	Rees Campbell	37
Static	Kate O'Neil	38
Referendum Night	Roslyn McFarland	39

Shattered Dreams	Dianne Kennedy	40
New Year Resolution	Robyn Mathison	41
Noise and a Voice	William Cotter	42
Selective hearing	Helga Jermy	43
Who Listens?	Adrianne K Wood	44
NO	Donna Edwards	45
Who?	Nance Cookson	46
Grave	Avril Bradley	47
with Oodgeroo Noonuccal	Jen Gibson	48
The Tragedy of Indigenous Australia	Ian McFarlane	49
elusive	Virgil Goncalves	50
For a Moment	Catharine Steinberg	51
Requiem for a Voice	Anne-Marie Smith	52
The Voices	Margaret Bradstock	53
afterwards 15 October 2023	Colleen Keating	54
My Boomerang Never Came Back	Brenda Saunders	55
Cinquain for the Future	Diana Pearce	56
2020 and beyond	Joan Fenney	57
Aqua Nullius	Gabrielle Journey Jones	58
Red sands	Maureen Mendelowitz	59
belonging	Millicent Jones	60
Truth	Mary Pomfret	61
In the 1950s	Alice Shore	62
Crying in the Wilderness	Jacqui Merckenschlager	63
Culling	Max Merckenschlager	64
Past and Future	Adrian Rogers	65
This Land	Rose Helen Mitchell	66
'left me awake'	Geoffrey Aitken	67
Grandma chat	Maryanne Sanders	68
revolution	Rory Harris	69
Australian Banyan	Melinda Jane	70

Truth Be Told	Allan Lake	71
Holdfast Bay	Airlie Jane Kirkham	72
Vigil	M.E. Berkley	73
Reactions	Joanna van Kool	74
Cape Grim 1828	Yvonne Adami	75
Marrickville Park	Josh Merten	76
Who Were the First?	Steve Davis	77
Ghost Gum Dwellers	Jennifer Chrystie	78
Closing Gaps, Opening Minds	Maurits Zwankhuizen	79
Confusion	Helene Castles	80
Jindalba	John O'Connell	81
Up the Gulf	David Cookson	82
Dark Australia	Susan Fitzgerald	83
Invasion	Rosalind Flatman	84
Medley: In the Beginning, the Dreaming	Mark Miller	85
Stuff you can buy now and soon	PS Cottier	86
More than sartorial	Sandra Renew	87
Unceded	Kate Maxwell	88
Walk in the Wind	Helen Budge	89
The sands by day, the desert stars by night	Jena Woodhouse	90
Whitsunday he came	Julie Maclean	91
Bunurong Eagle's Nest	Adèle Ogiér Jones	92
Turning Barrel	Geoff Graetz	93
Country	Robert Dickins	94
Advance Australia	Raymond Evans	95
This is Jenn & this is Eva as one	Rodney Williams	96
history bites hard	Adrian Flavell	97
Truths in Distant Times	Nicholas Hasluck	98
Such is Life	Anthony Mills	99
Ghost Gum	Jules Leigh Koch	100

from A Tasmanian Epic Poem	Graeme Hetherington	101
Pie-oneers	Andrew Drake	102
Pantoum for Uluru: 25 October 2019	Sue Aldred	103
settler's debt	Indrani Perera	104
Faded – reflections no. 2	David Taylor	105
Black Rights	Antonia Reiseger	106
Time Capsule	Derek Baines	107
A metaphor for hope	Pip Griffin	108
This Storied Land	Philip Radmall	109
Contest	Michael Keating	110
We Did Not Know Then	Brenda Eldridge	111
Straightness	John Lowe	112
The Keeper	Jeannie Lawson	113
Sunday Drives	Helen Lyne	114
Not One In a Hundred	Gillian Telford	115
In Whose Name?	Michelle Brock	116
Blood Orange Crown	Jude Aquilina	117
Glamping	Mary Jones	118
Pool of Tears	Jayne Linke	119
2 p.m. Sunday, 6 July 1835	Danny Gardner	120
Australian Horizon	Carolyn Gerrish	121
Threshold	Julie Thorndyke	122
First Farms	Paul Williamson	123
In the Glare	Kathryn Fry	124
For a Young Australian	Andrew Leggett	125
Dear River Authorities	Julie Birch	126
Plaited History	Margo Poirier	127
Four Generations	Jeanette Woods	128
Fearful	David Meldrum	129
After the Referendum 2023	Helen Swain	130

Introduction

This collection had its beginnings in the shame, sadness and disbelief that was felt by many after the result of the Voice referendum in 2023.

The poems here passionately express those reactions and also unflinchingly explore some of the truths about Australia and its history that, if they had been more widely known, might have led to a different result.

I hope readers will find solace, inspiration and hope in the pages that follow.

Stephen Matthews

Perhaps, After All, There is Hope

Famously, Auden said,
'Poetry makes nothing happen.'
We've heard this all too often;
It has become drained of meaning,

Like Keats' 'negative capability',
Which we've also heard too often.
But what does it mean?
Perhaps Auden didn't intend

To say, 'Poetry can't effect change.'
Let us hope so. Perhaps, magically,
He meant, 'Poetry makes Nothing happen.
It waves its wand and creates

'A Tinkerbell spangled space, a breathing
Air-lock, a screen on which
We may conjure affections,
A vacuum into which Nature

'Eagerly rushes with Natural Remedies.
It opens blocked paths. It lights lights.'
So that – yes – in fact, Poetry, *does*
Make places where change happens.

John Watson

Utopia

I dream of the day
when poets occupy the glass towers
        fill office high-rises
        working in shifts to translate
        an increasingly complex world.

I dream of the day
when new collections are headlines
        and old collections fill the shelves
        at airport bookshops
when poets are the only 'influencers'.

I dream of the day
when poets need to submit tax returns
        because they're poets
when effort rhymes with an hourly rate
when I can write 'poet' in the national census.

I dream of the day
when our poet laureate is the talking head
        everyone turns to for an opinion
when Hansard is condensed into haiku
when poems become policy.

Christopher Palmer

Dante's Lane

Dead English poets immortalised in street names
Addison/Shelley/Milton/Dickens/Elwood poet's corner
Wordsworth/Bronte threading a myth
through plane tree-lined streets
an English landscape covering
the shellfish cooked in middens
besides waterholes
fires burning on the bluff
signalling other clans
burning back country
pastures for kangaroos

newly named Dante Lane
a raging inferno a chilling symbol
untethered restitution
a snaked path of dry gum leaves
moss released from tidy constraint
an oyster's shell reborn as fungi growth
where spirits gather along the canal
Yalukit Willam clan
Boon Wurrung people
Eckermann/Oodgeroo/Birch/Coleman
succulent offshoots smile under the winter sun
Whittaker/Mudrooroo
a temperate wetland re-emerging

Mary Chydiriotis

Recipe for a Democracy Sausage

Take the entrails of a slaughtered pig, sheep or cow.
Better still, celebrate the triumphs
of western technology by choosing a sleeve
of cellulose, collagen or plastic.
Stuff the casing with the fat of the land,
the interests of tycoons and moguls,
and the demotic conspiracies
of online echo chambers.
Beef up your mince with the cankerous off-cuts
of the prime meats you could never afford.
Add a generous serve of artificial colours,
flavours and preservatives.
Tie at both ends then go cast your vote.

Return to the sizzling aroma of barbecued democracy.
Take, eat your treat with fried onion and tomato sauce
wrapped in white bread spread with marge.
Enjoy, secure in the knowledge that our country
has the fairest of all possible forms of governance,
and that tonight, when the pundits perform the auguries,
the sheer weight of numbers and formulae
will determine whose voices are to be heard
at the Table of Power. Have a nice day, now!

Anne Morgan

Lurch On

You didn't know
How the children
Secret issue of your fathers and torn from their mothers
Brutalised, pushed to the edges, humiliated and rejected
Were a test of your own humanity
You didn't know
The land you occupied was home to those who you denied
So that you may prosper

Work hard you said, if you wanna get ahead
But you refuse to recognise the pit holes in the playing field
Savages you said, even as you savage them
And primitive, because you heard someone else say it

You didn't know
That hurt and pain rain down as a result of colonisation
And the gap won't close on its own

Neither have you ever known First People
Seventy thousand years of culture on this continent
Cradle of humankind

You who chose not to know voted no and so
The Great Australian ignorance, the Great Australian shame
And the Great Australian pain, lurch on

Linda Wells

The Response, 14 October 2023

For J.

I'm watching but you can't look. The results roll in
like low, storm clouds. I'd expected some time to
settle in, but the commentator calls it about half
an hour into the broadcast. You can't listen even
though weeks before reports had opinion going
rapidly south. Who wanted to listen to the polls?
They've been wrong before, right? Someone else
tells me the whole thing is divisive. So, what's the
result called? Unifying?/ You can't sleep. Don't want
to talk about it. One week of silence. Reflection.
Mourning./ I take the Norfolk Island cone bursting
with seed scales and place them into soil. The seeds
will break their capsules perhaps remembering
their mother at Coogee Beach, and how the cone was
picked up by a stranger, put into a car and driven
to Queensland to become new trees. Seeds do what
Nature intends, break through the darkness. They do
what we all must do now: press on towards daylight.

Rosanna E. Licari

The Day the Voice Went Silent

after Frank O'Hara

It is 7.45 in Marrickville, Saturday
a day after Friday the 13th
in 2023 and we're turning up.
I stand in the morning sun
at the gate of Wilkins school, resisting sausages
and I hand out forms explaining how to vote
'It's not that hard, mate, just one word.'
And I chat with Dom who teaches in Parramatta
about tinfoil hats and racism and opportunistic lying
I walk home for juice
and peanut butter on toast and hot chocolate
Then I drive to St Nicolas' Church and stand
in the sun again and talk to James
and my son's ex-girlfriend who has just become an aunt
who arrives on her bike
and I hand out forms and tell people
which stairs to go up
and then I walk home and I
don't watch TV but
there's a text from my son
and I'm hearing Marcia
& Noel & Megan & Stan & Dean & Shane &
Pat & Linda and
remembering hope.

Jonathan Shaw

Sorry, no change

Tripping over tree roots
I went splat on the pavement.
In my palms, red poppies
bloomed instantaneously.
Nervous system in overdrive, I passed
Sue swaying her grandchild,
her husband dozing on the bench of the playground,
a fire truck, no flashing lights, another false alarm?
Remember how we tried to predict
the result of the referendum –
swinging like pendulums:
clockwise and counterclockwise.
I wanted to say something profound to her,
but with the verdict behind us
there was little point
we already knew what we had stood for
and what was now lost
so I kept on walking towards Centennial Park.
Along the circumference of a pond,
I could hear the breeze
trying to shift an entire world
I could sense the desperate dashing of
black, magnificent swans for a handful of breadcrumbs.

Real change is bloody hard.

Kavita Nandan

White speaks to black

Sorrows drift through the trees
like wraiths of winter mist.
How long, they sigh, *how long?*
You have lost many lifetimes
waiting to walk with us
to a shared future, but still
we continue to destroy the land
and alienate your people.

We have walked your one-time country
heedless of the interwovenness
of past and present, of land and people,
deaf to echoes of your feet and voices,
your songs and dances of deep learning.
Help us to find a shared future,
where we perceive the world you know.

You invited us to walk with you,
to join hands, hearts, and history,
to become, in time, one people.
But we were fearful, couldn't
comprehend or trust your vision.
So *still* you wait. But it *will* happen.
Many are ready to walk with you now,
and one day the others will follow.

Elizabeth Heij

An end of kindness?

They came to us gently
this dark-skinned people
voices soft and often
fading away, asked us
to give them a Voice to Government.

We came to them with muskets
which we fired above their heads…
Undeterred, and late in our history
they came to us with their request
a Voice to our Government.

By a resounding majority we spoke,
said No when they politely asked
for a Voice to Government.
No, no, no, no, no, no, no
in every state and community.

Will their patience run out
their gentle, soft approach
give way to anger, demanding
their rights? Will we then
fire right into their hearts?
Oh, no, please no!

Geoffrey Lilburne

Coloured by Disparity

Dark-skinned they are
racked by disease
and early death
while their children suicide

these bleak facts contrast
with the love in their souls
one that does not fade
for this red earth we claimed

they did not raise a gun
to demand their basic rights
palms open they have asked
we listen to their voice

with our genocide and greed
come lately to their land
we turned our backs
shut white ears, black hearts.

Michele Fermanis-Winward

Where can we go after 'No'?

Will all the hope, grace and promise
Of reconciliation go to waste?
Will politicians pack away their guilt,
Their lack of care, to let it moulder
In colonial cupboards and old reports?
Will it ever gather teeth again and re-emerge
In the next generation, or two or three?
Where will we hear the voice of collective shame?
Will it scream behind bars and bashings?
Will it fester silently in hearts and minds?
Will it ferment the poison of the past,
Hiding in the soul of the land,
Carried by wind to settle in water holes and caves,
Telling the story again and again?
Will it be soaked up by trees and grasses,
Tainting their growth, covering the earth
As they drop leaves and bark?
Will our shame lie dormant underfoot,
Trampled for generations?
Will it be lashed by fierce tides?
Can our collective shame be washed away
Or healed as the tide recedes?
How could we quash such hope,
Grace, promise, with one word?
Where can we go after 'No'?

Helen Seymour

It Takes Time To Know

for Pat Dodson, Linda Burney and many others

It takes time to know a people, their country,
And their past. There is much to see, to do
To listen for. A need to watch the seas, the skies,
Observe what moves and rests upon the land.

There are new words to hear, hands to touch,
Faces to be read to reach those private shores,
The mysteries of minds and waiting hearts
To be found at the deep centre of things.

You are new to these parts. Measuring our time
Living on these lands on a 24-hour clock, you arrived
Late in the day – ten minutes to midnight. Little time
To learn to watch the waves and ways of dreaming life.

We wished to write your name upon the sands,
To sing your stories with our ancient songs,
To be as one as sacred guardians of these lands
Together speaking truths and righting wrongs.

Surprised and saddened were we when you said No.
But we are a patient people, and we will go
On asking why you feared a friendly hand,
A voice to echo peace throughout this great land.

Maurice Whelan

Summertime in Australia

There's a glow in the summer air
a buzz of bees, the scent of lemon myrtle.
Blushing apples release crisp juice,
linger tart on the tongue.
A haze of smoky barbecue drifts past
shops which sparkle scarlet, gold, silver.
Santa waves from gardens and rooftops
floats bedecked crawl by to the jingle
of bells, the wave of upturned faces,
smiling masks suggestive of happiness.
Yet scrape the surface, rub off the facepaint
close the blinds, snuff out the candles.
There'll be no rejoicing here
while NO, rubs salt in open wounds
rejects once more the meek, the generous,
loses sight of love, of grace, of community.
Fears everyone but themselves.
Elsewhere, portents of the apocalypse
crawl ever closer shrouded in cloaks
of blood and tears, in howls of dog eat dog.
Kindness, trust, the joy of open arms
vanish into an abyss of hate and discontent.
Is this to be our future?

Mandy Toczek McPeake

Can we be one and free?

for all Australia's
given and could give us still
we are grateful now

birds sing, call through trees
their habitat now restored
creek flows by freely

we are one and free
land of the fair go for all –
disinformation

music *en plein air* –
homeless people in the park
move their tents closer

culture lost
child's ignorance – adult learning
culture uncovered / discovered

I apologise
for the truth that was not heard
can we still be friends?

Writing from the Heart

Members Carol McDonough, Elizabeth Delbridge, Julienne Webb,
Christina Kirkpatrick, Kerin Wanstall and Katy Gerner

Colony

Based on racism fed by greed
Our way is the norm 'other' inferior
Our way is the best without question
Our 'god given duty' to impose it

        From Invasion to Voice
        'Other' as lesser
        Nullius. No one. Nothing. No!

No one was here (no one like me)
No! – Don't know, don't care   enough to find out
Not my problem, nothing in it for me
After 200 years all we offer   is crumbs from the table

Hey! We'll have a say about whether to give you   a say!
Open that door (that door to your country)
Open that door   the tiniest chink

Of course it's non-binding we can choose to refuse
Still too much for the colonial mindset
        Nullius. No one. Nothing. No!

Karen Throssell

From the Heart of a Rock

This sun-burnt country –
Shapeless before your body's pain
Formed from the rainbow in drops of rain.

I felt alone in the ochre dust
Ants marvelled, insects crawled;
But I longed for the human breath:
Wild winds howled
In the crevices
Of my heartbeats.

I kept changing my colour
Sometimes I felt old but not broken.

I thought you might hear voices
And give the children a grace
Found in their songlines in every place.

In the darkness of the heart
whispers remain unheard:
But in my heart's cracks
A blackbird is building its nest.

The stunned sun still shines on me –
A bit scarred, but sacred in its silence.

In the heart of my grief
There's growing a green leaf…

Satendra Nandan

Post referendum observation

I love to see them strut –
those self-important gentlemen
garbed in black and white,
feathers glinting in the noonday sun.
They waddle over grass,
check to scavenge lawn grubs,
then condescend to come
to lunch with us outdoors.
Wary approaches.
One, more confident,
draws close, cocks head to side,
considers, hesitates, then,
in a swift advance, pecks crumbs
from outstretched hands
before a fast retreat.

At least these politicians are prepared
to take a risk. Trusting, they do not reject
the generous offering made
in hope of reconciliation
and belief that friendships can be forged.

Valerie Volk

no Voice as yet

of our total voting population
over seven million Australians
voted YES to add
a First Nations Voice
to our constitution

it's a relief to know
seven million Australians
are not fearful of losing their backyards
are not racist
are not selfish

how do seven million Australians
walk forward together
to reconciliation
with our First Peoples
when ten million compatriots
are afraid to

Ray Tyndale

Uluru Games of the Heart

We played 'Hide and Seek'
sought our soul, hid the truth.
'Coming, ready or not…' white leader said.
Too late. Soul, truth, both already dead,
some gave up the game, didn't play fair.
What to do now, soul-searchers, truth seekers,
how do we reconcile all in this land?
Not hostile, nor vengeful, the First People here,
but can they be happy, when cheated again?
Too often imprisoned, impoverished, hungry
their only freedom, freedom to dream.
Their children, not stolen, but often neglected,
yearning for learning in a language their own.
And what of ex-soldiers, shunned and ignored?
Pacifist patriots fighting for country, serving our creed.
These people came first, but it's no longer their country.
We've already said 'sorry', what more do they need?
Let them dream of the soil, the stars and the rivers,
the moon and the sun, the trees and the leaves.
But weep for our nation still hiding the truth,
we weep for the lies and seek shame for white thieves.

Janet Upcher

The Forgotten Voices of Australia

Rustle *Balga* grasstree, breeze shuffling your monocot
Galgawari RUN! *Jahdjam*-child RUN! Quickly…
Mubarn Maaman come now in uniform and black car
Streaked tears stain little faces, wide-eyed, FEAR!
Desperate, cling, claw at Mothers shoulders, TERROR!
Arms up! Little hands up! Grasping DESPERATE!
White *yirahli* yanks *jahdjam*-child into car, SCREAMS!
Mother drops to the dusty dirt track, WAILS!
Arms clutching chest, deep pain in her ribs, FRENZY!
Oblivious to stones cutting deep into knees
Sisters *b'long* her, hold her, blood oozes into red soil!
Distraught heads throw back, wail in agonising grief
Clutch at one another, wreathing on ground like snakes
Screams muffled, by laughter from black car engine
Voices lost in the wind, as *mulgar*-thunder rolls…
Klari-lizard observes from nearby fiery rock…
Their voices lost in the blood in the soil…
On an adjoining cattle station, black girl is broken in
She is ringers' boy, they call her *Waddagal*-wild dog
This one is *karnya*-shame, spirited, kicks up dust
Ringer drags her by the hair, roped behind his horse
Yoorn-goanna lazing near a dying campfire, watches!
Voices forgotten when human invaded *Flora and Fauna's* land
Uliva-Beware! Better NO Give tortured voices a platform
What narratives they might push IF they had *a Voice*.

Deborah Anne Tanzer

The vote

They stand in line
                looking ahead
        wearing silence as a shield
        their clothes drab
alongside yellow   red   blue
                  posters
            claiming omniscience

There is a gauntlet to be run
        hard-eyed creatures
                effusing congeniality
        offering insistence
                stamped onto paper sheets

Inside the sanctuary
        bureaucratic smoothness
                lubricates process

Simple pencil strokes
                two letters or three
        squarely imprisoned
the force able
                to slash the hearts
        of our countrymen
                and the nation's face

Greg Tome

'Straya, no worries

'Straya is watching
                the cricket
                the footy
                the tennis
                and the golf
                no stress
'Straya is
                on the beach – tanning
                in the pub – guzzling
                at the gym – pumping
                no dramas

'Yes' vote fails
                chill bro'
'70 Australian women murdered in 2023'
                all good
'Nazis on the trains'
                too easy

'Straya, mate, it is what it is

John Bartlett

Australia's Referendum on the Voice

They called it the Voice
we all have a voice, but how do we reconcile
a nation's ideal of equality for all?
Let's strip it back to the bare bones
to how those who came from Europe
viewed its original inhabitants
Today we call them First Nations peoples
a blanket term covering an underlay of atrocities
dispossession, theft, slavery, abuse, stolen generations

Haunted winds still hold the grief of the Black Line
Christian missions, poisoned water holes, murdered families
Maralinga, prison cells, deaths in custody –
and in those haunted winds the answer lies

Aboriginals are guardians of our land
they hold an earthbound philosophy
stretching back through time into our modern world
the land provides their every need
from it they come, and to it they shall return
they are the voice of ancient wisdom
people and land co-existing in mutual sacredness
If we could understand and cherish this mutual sacredness
it might save all of us from ourselves

Thérèse Corfiatis

referendum

they relax back
into dreamtime stories
and take solace
away from the biting whip
of voting results

Dawn Bruce

Terra Nullius

Through the spyglass they gazed from ship to shore
where campfires joined with stars to light the night.
An obvious truth was spun into the biggest lie –
Terra nullius was claimed over two centuries ago,

to describe the vast ancient southern land –
a land that belonged to no one.
A land occupied for more than sixty thousand years
by people who never ceded their sovereignty.

Since invasion there have been frontier wars,
stolen generations, incarceration and more.
This year, those first people offered our nation
the *Uluru Statement from the heart*.

It was a gift, a hand to heal the rift.
When will our icy hearts thaw enough
to shed our mantle of mean spiritedness
and embrace truth, make reparation?

We know, *No No* short-sighted stunts
created fear and a swift *No* vote.
Post referendum we retreat to burrows, feel our sorrow,
until again we have choice, to walk as one with voice.

Liz Newton

Voiceless

They asked us for a voice. Just a voice…
not our backyard, not our families,
not even the keys to our jails.

They invited us to walk with them
towards a land where sovereignties could co-exist
where truth could flourish, and gaps could close.
They braved our ignorance
they faced our racism
trusted in friendship, our compassion in compromise.

But we were led by fear, by greed, by belief in all
the fallacies, the conspiracies, the downright lies
we downplayed as misinformation.
We obfuscated, prevaricated, confused and muddied…
Listened instead to the politics of power

We wouldn't accept advice from them, those 3 per cent
who came from and with the land we now call our own.

So if we won't listen, and if we won't walk together…
will the disunity, discord and disdain wave engulf us?

Must they weep in silence?

Rees Campbell

Static

Sorry,

but we can't hear you.
What are you trying to say?
You'll have to speak up –
there's a lot of interference
for some reason.
What have you lost? Choice?

Oh, your voice, is it?
That does make things difficult.
Perhaps we should try again later,
what with your having no voice
and our having such poor reception.
So long,

Sorry.

Kate O'Neil

Referendum Night

We were there from the beginning
of the ABC's referendum coverage, watching
Antony Green, grim-faced on our 65-inch smart TV,
predict early a win for the NO campaign. But even so
I hoped it was a kind of faltering, stuttering no
like the no, no, no of the dim-witted Jim of Dibley,
that was really a yes. But no!
In truth it was a clear and clean kind of no –
as hearty as a lout's whistle, as boisterous as
a big brass band but as brutal and precise as a Pilbara
explosion blasting sacred sites into oblivion. It was
a who-do-you-bloody-well-think-you-are kind of no.
I don't have a voice, so why should you? Your tales
of woe don't wash with me. I'm sick of hearing you
whinge. Just shut up and get on with it.
That was the kind of no it was. A no to possibility.
A no to justice. A denial of the violent human history
of our sunburnt, wide brown land.
Ugly lies had won the day.

Having no words, we switched off the screen,
plunging the room into silent darkness – not yet proud
of being part of the 40% who voted YES.

Roslyn McFarland

Shattered Dreams

June rains had washed the russet face
leaving the rock refreshed in the sun
in hope we prayed it was an omen
of better things soon to come
but truth and justice again were dashed
by misinformation and stories untrue
voters made the choice to give no voice
shattering dreams created at Uluru.
Tears rippled down elders' cheeks
from Torres Strait to remote towns
but bravely they rallied and sadly said
it was not the first time they had been let down.
First whites told lies of *terra nullius*
which led to slaughter, poisonings and pain
no mercy was shown across the land
indigenous children and babes were slain
or torn away from those they loved
whose lives became consumed with sadness
and sacred sites fell to white man's greed
and are lost still in their heartless madness.
Official recognition and reconciliation
in this country are long overdue
the most just way to right this wrong is to heed
the sincere pleas from the heart
set down at Uluru.

Dianne Kennedy

New Year Resolution

I am now eighty-five years old,
daughter of a curly-haired,
'olive-skinned', stolen
Aboriginal child.

She loved poetry,
read and recited it to her children.
Kath Walker and Faith Bandler
were heroines of hers.

Since the referendum
in October 2023,
I have been almost paralysed
with grief and despair.

I must pick up my pen,
write to members of parliament,
demand truth-telling and treaty –
be a voice for the voiceless.

Robyn Mathison

Noise and a Voice

We have seen the stirring ad.
We have heard the words,
The unfaltering rhythm.
Seen, in front of the famous Bridge,
The drummers standing precise as robots
And the well rehearsed dancers.
Seen and heard,
In a Time-gnawed, iconic gorge,
A multicultural choir
Singing, hands joined together,
We are One and We are Many,
Then adding, as if in triumph,
We are Australian
And we drink to our success,
Our giving of a voice to all.
But, then, we torpedo,
Without remorse and with great efficiency,
Any plan to give our First Peoples
A place in our constitution
Or a path to addressing our Parliament.

William Cotter

Selective hearing

sea fog
over colonial port…
referendum lost

        pademelon
        stunned in a ditch

a hundred voices
to every four first nations'…
our hearing impairment

weather report
storms all over the world
wren song on the fence

        galahs bleeding through sky
        too late, too late

the road ahead
mountain top hidden in cloud
a steep climb

Helga Jermy

Who Listens?

Long ago, my ancestors were forced to
cultivate often barren and hostile places,
driven off their farms for landlord's profits,
settling in far away lands,
conscripted into brutal wars for the Empire
which had displaced them.
There are those, high up or lowdown,
left wingers or right,
who would smother every breath we
take or words we speak or write,
regardless of gender,
race or long ago country of origin.
The solitary moon shines overhead
like a beacon for travellers in the dark.
The moon is a symbol of all
the written word down the ages,
that illuminates our thought, and choices.
All people on planet earth are of inherent worth.
However, there are too many towns with no pity.
No one shares, no one cares and no one hears.
We all have a voice but WHO LISTENS?

Adrianne K Wood

NO

such outback sadness
girt by seasoned brittle shards of unkindness

Donna Edwards

'No' was the loud and clear outcome of the 2023 referendum to acknowledge First Nations people in the Australian Constitution and to seek a voice in parliament about matters affecting them.

Who?

And who will stir the pudding
of memories of the past
to blend with promises to come
the question begs an answer to be sure

Count the blessings
count the sorrows
and all of the tomorrows
then think again before you close the door

Nance Cookson

Grave

I look to the future
see only a recurrent
past. No lessons learnt.
The distance we make
between others with
bigger and better
weapons of destruction.
Kindness destroyed by vote.
It is like grief
this rejection and
I must ask why, why
did it happen.
Humanity buried
under self-importance.

Avril Bradley

with Oodgeroo Noonuccal*

We carry 'No' in shame and fear today. While
YES gives voice to life that's clear of
bigotry and bitter shouts,
'No' wants to answer, 'That's all lies.'

'Let no one say the past is dead.
The past is all about us and within.'*

In realms of quantum qubits Time's not
linear, while Space's scale of tragi-comedy is
limitless.

Yet Truth is here – no matter 'when', waiting nearby
beyond our present ken. In hope-filled grace let's
soon embrace as sisters in a happier place.

No victories are to be won, till
Australians we engage as One.

Jen Gibson

* Oodgeroo Noonuccal, aka Kath Walker, *My People*, Jacaranda Press, 1970

The Tragedy of Indigenous Australia

For fifty thousand years or more
this land was theirs alone –
songlines cast from Dreamtime,
and nurtured at the bone.

Until a hungry Empire
judged their ancient world
to have no sovereign power
without its flag unfurled.

And so, a colony began,
with prejudice and haste,
intent on federation
and disrespectful waste.

To reach a global context
with multicultural choice,
while denying the Indigenous
a parliamentary voice.

Ian McFarlane

elusive

is there any point, any longer, to truth,
the wise woman muses, when it seems
as unattainable as clutching a cloud in the

present
era of fake photos, scare tactics or one-liner lies.

the point is, she ponders, unless we always
try to seek truth,
nobody would know what happened in the

past
(if massacres took place, if children were stolen)
nor how the

future
is intended
(if new referendums fail, if voices are forever lost).

so, she concludes, there's always
a point to searching for truth
until we find it – and, once we do,
it needs to be clutched, like a cloud,
even if fleetingly, to our hearts.

Virgil Goncalves

For a Moment

For a moment in time
The old folk appear

Silent souls
Listening
To stories on Country
Witnesses
To loss, grief
And unrequited love
The circle of kin
Draws close
Around the living
Pulsating flesh
Of family
Sharing Dreamtime
Sacred knowledge
A song
A dance
A voice

Time opens
Time closes

The moment is lost
Along with the ancestors

Catharine Steinberg

Requiem for a Voice

after François Villon's Ballade *Frères humains qui après nous vivez*, 1489

Sisters among whom I've enjoyed living,
Those of you whose words I have read and heard,
Women who ponder the choices we have,
My daughters (and those later born of them),
Sisters be aware, you are role models
Forget the crude jests and crass abuses
That mocked you and your personal beliefs
The Uluru call was a people's cry
Own your power and claim: kulila!*
People, be humane: listen to the voice.

Australians, your First Peoples have spoken
Asking for their growth to be supported,
Calls for survival have remained unheard
Can't we offer them the chance of progress?
Ignore the put-downs rebukes and the likes
Yesterday we closed and maintained silence,
We switched off the news, respecting elders
Let's be heard again, speak for a fair go!
Grant the First Peoples what they ask, be just!
People, be humane: listen to the voice.

And you good reader, wishing to alleviate
The First Peoples' needs in healthier days,
You who plan ahead devising programs
For a better life, take a step: be kind!
People, be humane: listen to the voice.

Anne-Marie Smith

kulila: means 'listen!' in Pitjantjatjara language in the APY lands

The Voices

Across the blue horizon, looking out towards
        Ben Buckler, where elite glassed-in mansions
overhang the rocky headland, you may dream
    of ownership, knowing nothing of its namesake.

You might have seen surfers, body-boarding
        in the breakers, heedless of tsunami warnings
in that curve of empty beach,
        heard tourists walking past your window
shouting, laughing, tossing drink cans,
            footsteps running.

*

From Port Jackson through the bushlands, Eora
        fleeting softly to well-known fishing spots,
      (bark canoes upon their heads)
          left shellfish middens, stone spearheads,
            at the edges of the dunes.

In the flat sea cliff, a place called Murriverie
            rock carvings record the story,
species of fish, an early shark attack,
           the platforms now blistering,
      poorly drained, eroded,
ancestral pathways fading
        in caverns of the mind.

Margaret Bradstock

afterwards 15 October 2023

it is as if a forest gapes   exposed
sky often so blue growling grey
pungent air stifling breath
as if fire has devoured Country
ground of tiny orchids (gifts
of grace) gnashed in grief
questions sear like scars burnt
into memory
the tongues of eucalypts (that
i always understand) are tied in foetal
knots and a great silence falls over the land

the fall of tears like rain absolve
the blackened trunks of iron barks and
eucalypts cut the shadow side of beauty
slowly the howling wind softens
forest is heard with hymn of
yellow-green whispers
don't despair of being the witness
spirit is not spent
the tongues of eucalypts (that
i always understand) unfurl naked   sore
their sap murmurs *today we begin again*

Colleen Keating

My Boomerang Never Came Back

I aimed high
Sent authority
Flying over clouds
Of injustice
Wisdom and patience
Burnt in the wood

Watched the sky
For acceptance
Someone
To throw it back
Cross the fields
Of ignorance

Found it labelled
Artefact
Strength and purpose
Boxed
In the museum
Of indifference

Brenda Saunders
Wiradjuri Nation

Cinquain for the Future

Yesterday
bereft   lost
dispossessing   stealing   ignoring
one-eyed views only recorded
yesterday.

Tomorrow
clear-eyed   receptive
peace-making   truth-telling   unifying
all people linked as one
tomorrow.

Diana Pearce

2020 and beyond

after the opening paragraph of *A Tale of Two Cities* by Charles Dickens

…it was the worst of times
it was a time of wonder, it was a time of disbelief
it was the age of wariness,
                it was the age of recklessness
it was the season of new breath,
                it was the season of choking
it was the autumn of possibilities,
                it was the winter of grief

we had everything before us, we had nothing before us
we drifted into chaos
                we locked down with the familiar
we were promised freedom, we were kept enclosed
we longed to move, we were scared to leave
we lost those we cherished, we birthed new arrivals
we connected with loved ones,
                we were distant from others

it was a time we looked inwards,
                it was a time we looked afar
it was a time of renewal, it was a time of depletion
it was a time that defined us,
                it was a time of confusion
it was a time with no ending,
                it was the past and the present

Joan Fenney

* lines in italics from *A Tale of Two Cities*

Aqua Nullius

First Nation families
Custodial responsibilities
Care-taking waterways
Respectfully farming the sea
Attuned to ancient knowledge
60,000 years of offshore technology
Aqua Nullius is a fallacy.

Interconnecting ecologies
Flowing from mother mountains
Rivers and lakes to sacred beaches
Delicately woven on Yuin Country
Thrived under traditional administration
Aqua Nullius is a fallacy.

Communing with the moon
Travelling Thaua tides
Fishing the whale road
Casting the strong salty nets
Of their ancestors deep and wide
Gathering sustenance for the tribe
With gratitude and balance
For all that the ocean provides.
Aqua Nullius is a fallacy.

Gabrielle Journey Jones

Red sands

Long shadows fall on waterways
        and reach the rugged heights
Footprints lean on pebbles
        and print across red sands
Clicks and bird cries
        darting eyes
Haunting calls
        across the land
Knowing seeing
        hearing feeling
        dreaming
        recalling
        smoking
        dancing

We've sliced the fabric
We've pierced the loin
        We'e severed the sinews
        and splintered the bone

We've cut down forever
        the ancient past

        the ancient people
        in this ancient land

Maureen Mendelowitz

belonging

this is my land
nobody owns this land
but it is mine and all
who give their hearts to it –
if you belong to it, it is yours.
It is yours if your tears dwell with
the grace of the eagle gliding
above an endless horizon
yes it is my land
and all generations
who have walked hand in hand
through the distant dawn over red
earth and spinifex into the mystery
of gold and darkening skies –
and all generations who have
bravely journeyed here
in schooners, chains or planes –
it is my land, it is yours to
watch over and cherish – our island,
this land of time – its snowy peaks and
tossing shores that whisper secrets
from the past: let us live freely,
free from resentment, to
sing our song
of being one.

Millicent Jones

Truth

To tell you the truth they would still be living
Like bloody savages if it wasn't for us.
I mean what could people be doing with themselves
For 60,000 years or more if they weren't busy making
Bombs or money or digging for gold? Who knows?
Maybe they busied themselves making bush bread
From seeds or carved a didgeridoo or two
(the world's oldest wind instrument) from hollowed out
Stringy bark or knocked up return flight boomerangs
Without foreknowledge of the complicated principles of
Aerodynamics and asymmetrical lift.
Maybe they even wasted time inventing thermoplastic
Resin strong enough to bind wood to rock
Or creating complex canal systems for fish farms
Or mucking about with fire-stick farming
And bush medicine to heal and protect their own.
Maybe they even lolled around crafting stone
Tools as sharp as any colonist's knife and necklaces
Of tiny shells that shone as bright as trading beads.
They didn't achieve much at all really did they?
Lucky for them we came along to save them.
And isn't that the truth?

Mary Pomfret

In the 1950s

Saturday arvos, we white kids,
terriers racing for rabbits ahead,
roamed free the hills around the Sturt Gorge.

But there was something chilling in the Gorge dankness,
disturbing us under the huge rock overhang
when we scuffed sand edging the river.

And up at Colebrook Children's Home,
the stolen black children whiled their time,
kicking footballs or sitting on the steps,
staring westwards beyond the high barbed fence
defining their allotted space.

Alice Shore

Crying in the Wilderness

We took the children away, away from a dying race.
We took the children away to save their souls for God.
We stole the children from grieving mothers
And told them she didn't care.

We take the children away to protect our civil society.
We punish their wanton ways by locking them in gaols.
Children as young as ten are crying in darkness
Locked in cells for all but an hour a day.

And now we ask them to accept – they have
No voice, no hope of acceptance, no hand of friendship
Despite their deeply considered and generous proposal
They are spurned by the hard of heart
Rejected in their own land.

Jacqui Merckenschlager

Culling

Lets mount for the hunt!
Our quarry walks the plains
the thrill of a chase
is coursing through my veins.
Domestics are safe
they're paddocked with the stock
but ferals outside
are destined for a shock.
We'll cut out the young
they're wily and they're fast
make them first your mark
the old and frail will last.

To echoing wails
of blackmen in the night
the wails from domestics
on witnessing the plight
the wailing of kinsmen
in keening for their lost
the culling shall end
but never will the cost.

Max Merckenschlager

Past and Future

We came as strangers,
a young people
to an old world
confronting dangers
not always willingly
but pioneering,
persevering,
often misunderstanding
ancient sanctities
attitude and entities
with which we were
at time conflicted
when from a wider world
we were hurled – into
a maelstrom of change
testing our range,
at times constricted
but taught by a land
that might make, break,
or become our future,
re-creating us to bear,
aspire to, even dare,
a destiny.

Adrian Rogers

This Land

The mighty McDonnell Ranges
blazed and bellowed
'Notice me'
Standing beside me,
a young Aboriginal
park ranger,
asked my opinion
of the scenery.
I turned to face her.
I stood stock-still.
Two deep blue eyes,
blue as the blanket of sky above us,
and sprinkled with glinting stars,
they echoed the sparks of silver
in her clear brown cheeks,
and punctuated the scene with a
historical touch of Ireland.

Rose Helen Mitchell

'left me awake'

for Oodgeroo Noonuccal

she is going
with her story

somewhere quieter
perhaps
where the darkness
is far warmer

than European
brightness

flashed as white light
so terrifyingly discourteous
it only recommended departure.

i wish i might know
where silence still disturbs her

Geoffrey Aitken

Grandma chat

Magpies warble this isn't just barbie banter
two aged stripped to the honest core
of bare bones truth telling;
Grandma Rita, black as a starless night,
a breath of ancient lineal trace back
Grandma Emmy with hybrid ancestral lines,
a white migrant in the Oz melting pot mix
those two share their heartfelt dreamings,
their early years, both barefoot infants outdoor
make your own fun in the dust play kids
ghostly white gums for Rita.
Hidden springs in gorge chasms
hunting trips for bush tucker
kangaroos, wallabies and bush bugs
tracing tracks, remembering, remembering
ancestral hunting grounds, waterholes.
For Emmy, river-studded countryside, green swaths
horse riding in the open, carefree explorations
seasonal farm chores assisting Farmer Tom
grandchildren of dust ladies, nurtured by Mother Nature
both fizzing with the wrench of grandmotherly love
carriers of the ancestral spirits.
They pray each grandchild
can learn about the other, about their home Australia
hold their heads up high
and be someone

Maryanne Sanders

revolution

The dark suits of colonisation
a heavy tread through country

a bouquet of colour will always win
the canvas of the heart a luxury

Rory Harris

Australian Banyan

Rhinoceros skin
Elephant trunk
Roots like clown feet.

Buttress, intricate mess
Your splayed fingers, saluting
Shooting towards nirvana.

At your base
Snake-shapes gather
Like a necklace
Or clothing-apparel.

Indigenous people; your epitaph
'Becoming Banyan'.

We, strangler fig, germinate
Wrap arms to stabilise base.

We take sustenance, as
We stretch, we suffocate host tree.

Indigenous people; your epitaph
'Banyan'.

Melinda Jane

Truth Be Told

The Idyllic Period on the continent
now known as Australia – as on all
continents – was pre-homo sapien
so a long, long, long, long time ago.
Blue heron ate blameless little fish.
This marsupial killed and ate that
marsupial but payback killings
were unknown, abuse of the female
half of a species was unknown,
tribal warfare unknown.
As history – including fiction – attests,
that's just part of what we sapiens are,
whether on a small or industrial scale.
We arrive and art…and the art
of war comes along for the ride.
Of course there may be a 2nd Idyllic
Period should we become extinct
but in the meantime hope for better
but expect the usual meanness.

Allan Lake

Holdfast Bay

A dusty land, native trees, untouched sandy shore
greeted those pioneers who landed
in Holdfast Bay long ago.
I stand in awe of them.
What did they think of their new home, the Bay?

Recall their fortitude as powerful men
proclaimed ownership of this new land.
Hardship, flies, lack of food,
sunburn, malicious mozzies, all no more.
What would they now think of the Bay?

No more mud houses. Pristine sands, high-rise hotels,
the dusty lanes replaced by tram tracks.
Ice cream parlours, coffee and cake shops,
nice chocolate nooks, and bustling boutiques.
How could they have foreseen such a futuristic Bay?

No expectation of such a forlorn place
becoming a civic community, of holiday makers,
revellers, commercialisation, shopping till you drop.
The awesome beauty of their environment,
their once new life at the Bay gone forever,
but always remembered.
Would they be happy or sad with today's Bay?

Airlie Jane Kirkham

Vigil

A candle for my sisters,
Harmed as I have been,
By him whose weapon hands and wolf teeth
Shredded safety and stole from deepest places
Secrets passed mother to daughter
Since Eve's fateful bite.

A candle for my mother,
Acquaintance of harm.
Sought refuge in her salted words
Sung into my wound:
'Hush, child, this is the way of the man.
Speak not of it and it will not grow.
Think not of it and they will not know.
They cannot give you what you seek.
It is for us, in private, to weep.'

A candle for my daughter,
Beloved dream I cannot have.
Burdened of knowledge, what right have I
To steal her soul from heaven, plant here on Earth
Perfect marble carved by harmful hands
Crying in the night, echoing for eternity
Unheard.

M.E. Berkley

Reactions

She sits across the road
from the bus stop; stares out
at the passing parade,
'Should get a proper job; have a shower,
 lazy bitch; and you'll notice
she can afford smokes
so she must do all right on the dole.'
I realise the man seated next to me wants a response,
but I can find nothing to say
that wouldn't seem rude
so I half smile and look straight ahead.

It's cold sitting here where the sun doesn't reach
and the slats of the seat are uncomfortably hard.
I think of the warmth of home and my cat
curled up on the chair waiting for me.
What does she eat when the day fades to dusk?
How far to a loo and maybe a tap?
Does she snuggle down in her blanket
at night? Find some warmth?
When people pass by they tend to ignore
the uncomfortable truth of such lives
while I long to be home in the warm with a wine
to shrug off this scene and leave it behind.

Joanna van Kool

Cape Grim 1828*

The fragrance of earth
After rain
Dawn sweeps below
The granite ridge
Hangs in trees
Clings to creek water
With spear and net
Hunters walk the shoreline
In salt and wind
Gather shearwater

A bank of cloud
Shadows the land
Gunshot
Breaks the silence
Men on horseback
Surround the hunters
They seek shelter
On the headland

The sea below
Wild and dark

The blood of life
On the tide eternal

Yvonne Adami

---

* The Cape Grim massacre was an attack on 10 February 1828 in which a group of Aboriginal Tasmanians gathering food at a beach in the north-west of Tasmania is said to have been ambushed and shot by four Van Diemen's Land Company workers, with bodies of some of the victims then thrown from a 60-metre cliff.

Marrickville Park

The thick-trunked jarrah with leaves like fraying silk
Breathes sounds like an ocean hushing
In dusty winter wind.
His slow-blinking eyes drip with green mist,
Lorca dormant on his knee
With tuneless songs.
I feel about buildings what I do trees.
I'm reminded how close I am to the ground.

The fountain is running again.
That man with ripped pants
And a cracked voice
Will be back soon
To wash.

Josh Merten

Who Were the First?

Who were the first to make a stand
defending this, our native land?
Their names are gone, their deeds unsung.
How many heads in shame are hung
when we who chant 'Lest we Forget'
(our fallen not forgotten yet)
have cenotaphs in every town,
but none for skin of black, or brown.
No treasured names of ancient warriors
cast on brass plaques to remind us,
we were once the hordes descending,
they their homelands were defending.
If there's a god and she is just,
we've wrongs to right, but first we must
grant as partial reparations,
now, their title, the First Nations.

Steve Davis

Written before the term First Nations became generally accepted

Ghost Gum Dwellers

Banyule Wetlands, heartland of the Wurundjeri-willam

Fire lures fish to the point of my spear
white fires run so fast they kill our living
fire streams from mountain tops

We dig daisy roots with red gum sticks
white men pierce earth's skin for houses
earth cracks wide, swallows the lot

We gather the wattle's sweet sap
our dingoes ooze blood from bullet holes
springs gush from hot rocks

We pound grass seeds for flour, white dogs
chew our bones, suck the marrow
stones grind stones in rivers of ice

Jennifer Chrystie

Closing Gaps, Opening Minds

Let's honour what society forgets:
There is much left that we can still put right;
Throw boomerangs instead of epithets,
Blow caves with ochre, not with dynamite.

Let's live in tune with nature, not against it,
Seeing the land as kindred, not a slave,
Walking each songline (where they haven't fenced it),
Digging a deadly life, no early grave.

Worship the earth, not economic creed,
Embracing harmony instead of violence,
Respecting finite life, not endless greed,
And offer welcomes, though receiving silence.

We must close cultural awareness gaps,
Not just the ones whitefellas measure by;
Engage with art and nature, not just apps,
And then there'll be more chance to unify.
We all can help to heal this land's collapse,
Which we in two short centuries bled dry.

Maurits Zwankhuizen

Confusion

Loss floats like a cloud
in the space above each letter
hovers over an idea, words react,
capture the essence of reason,
a tenuous thinning thread.

Loose sands shift in the wind,
sands that ripple down,
drift over the page, blur the intent.
Words, now broken and slurred,
leave the message, unread.

Love cascades through the flow
of an errant stream of thought,
surges through deep pink
canyons of stone, emerges cleansed:
the outback sunset bleeds red.

Helene Castles

Jindalba

a legacy

majestic buttressed columns stretch up
and support the leafed canopy, listen
there is a soft clear call, wom-poo
high above the path wandering
through thousands of years
a rain-dampened red
leaf-littered earth
its ancient aroma
the hushed sounds
of the stream flowing
and cooling breeze drifting
in a sublime sunlit peacefulness
which speaks to us only of respect
for ourselves, for others, for the land

John O'Connell

Up the Gulf

A firebox flung open,
morning sweat stains the woman's T-shirt
flaunting her nation's emblem
as with bare feet she pads along the dirt verge.
Distant reflections prick the mirage
resolve into a road train
a saurian of clashing steel.
It bludgeons the heat haze
swaggers to stop beside her
in a stink of cattle shit
revs hard to shrug off its dusty skin.
The woman sneezes from the grime
pretends not to see the engine oil
dripping black, soiling that red earth;
nor the rig's kelpie snarling
with yellowed fangs –
those three colours a mocking echo
of her own, yet she walks on,
becomes the horizon
footprints barely perceptible
already blurred by the wind.

David Cookson

Dark Australia

Feet pound the dust
echoing through the millennia

Men glide with movements
transforming into kangaroo, emu, telling of the hunt

Dark bodies tell stories by firelight
under the clear sky of ancient days

Revealing the deeper truths
in the hearts of those watching

Chanting and sticks clacking join
the drone of didgeridoo

Way back they tell, way back
long before a white foot touched any soil

Way back they tell, way back
long before tall ships came with false claims

Way back, way way back, ancient lives in balance

Bring forward now
Bring forward for those who sorely need the equality

Susan Fitzgerald

Invasion

He kissed me as I wandered down the street,
yellow sun on black and red,
I want to marry you, he said, but I don't have the money,
well you'll just have to save up more, I said,
hugging arms, once stolen,
I want a white one, not a black,
not black, he said,
bemused, I floated home in my white cloud,
I hadn't asked him why,
that would have been rude.

Rosalind Flatman

Medley: In the Beginning, the Dreaming

1

Ngunnawal dawn –
freshly limned palm prints
on the cavern walls.

2

Sphagnum bog –
the untrampled trails
of Nunniong spirits.

3

Rock overhang –
out of the ashes the nutty paste
of bogong moths.

4

Campfire glow –
on cave walls the sacred tongues
of Wandjina figures.

5

Out of the mist
the flicker of ghost lights –
Dreamtime waterhole.

Mark Miller

Stuff you can buy now and soon

A mop with an extendable pole to remove spiders,
because hard-to-get spiders are a thing.
Special detergent to clean your dishwasher.
A $5 T-shirt made by really happy women,
in a country called Somewhere Else.
A robot who opens beer fluently
and says *G'day mate*.
He always puts his thumb up to show
that everything is always already fine.
Shares in lithium mines. Shares in AussieRobots.
(Their name is always given as OzRobs.)
New computers after the other newish one dies.
Pretend marbled red meat that really bleeds,
to pick out the more squeamish vegans.
(OzRob will clean your bloody dish,
or at least stack the ultraclean washer.)
An AI cricket match to project onto the wall
of your underground bunker. Books on wellness
which do not emphasise the 'we'.
A fake golden-shouldered parrot to ride
on the shoulder of your trusty OzRob,
who will adopt a piratic accent, if you wish.
And you do so wish, oh yes, most definitely, for
who doesn't love a pirate, parrot-epauletted?

PS Cottier

More than sartorial

during and after a ritual knotting of the tie
(choker, cravat, scarf, neckerchief, bow tie, ascot)
something undeniable happens –
we all know the history…we all see today's story
any knot's a tie knot, twist, loop, old knot, new knot
combinations, two knots or one knot
let's just use ordinary people knots –

power dressing since the seventeenth century
all those men, ordinary, but powerful, entitled,
vengeful, brought the necktie to Australia, were
tied in to dominate, impose their will on nations, land,
women – but when women flaunt a tie, apparently,
the tie is a penis, showing penis envy,
risks the wearer as a lesbian,
makes everyone uncomfortable

cross-dressing ambiguity loosens choke holds
but they're hanging on to power by their fingertips
twisting, swirling, tunnelling, snaking, flaring,
colonial, patriarchal, all our history in a choke hold
assume the mantle as the mirror is still reflecting
four hundred years of more than sartorial

Sandra Renew

Unceded

We travel to the heart
pulsing red   eternal
pockmarked   patterned with time
sighing dusty breath   more than five hundred
million years   into stretched desert blue.

Spinifex waves homage
to the sandstone monolith
mounting its one-fist-raised
challenge to the sky.
Black flies   cigarette butts   half-buried

tickets   cluster in the weedy corners
of the carpark   where tyres upon gravel
twitter of tourists   soundtrack
the sunlit curve   and unvoiced claim
of an arkose giant.

Later   from the viewing area
lovers   Japanese travellers
dancing arm in arm   and children
stirring creep of cold   with sparklers
laud the silent bleed   of a stony sunset.

Kate Maxwell

Walk in the Wind

A south wind pounds
the sea and me.
I breathe in and
the purging wind blows
out the bad and
the good flies in.
I think of
smoking ceremonies.
Walk with me.

Helen Budge

The sands by day, the desert stars by night

a villanelle

I bathe myself in ancient and excoriating light,
surrender to the cleansing of day's blinding rays,
the stars by night.

Now that we have massacred our spiritual guides,
we must wander godless in the trackless wastes:
I bathe myself in ancient and excoriating light.

The rituals they practised to protect the land have
ossified, or burned to ashes in the strangers' haste.
But no invader desecrates the stars by night.

The sanctity of nest and cradle, birthright, waning
like the moon; songlines fading, old cultures erased.
I bathe myself in ancient and excoriating light.

Premonitions of our doom cannot be put to flight;
the blood of innocents seeks justice in the blaze
of stars by night.

The sanctuary of nest and womb is antechamber
to the tomb, the ark is now too crowded to suffice;
I bathe myself in ancient and excoriating light –
the sands by day, the desert stars by night –

Jena Woodhouse

Whitsunday he came

Sailing through drowned mountains
known as *Whispering Sands*

by the seafaring Ngaro
Cook spots an old humpback

up from Antarctica
Whales hold memories of before,

when land was joined, pre-ice
and the big thaw

like old souls from the south
shifting north in the Great Migration

to coral isles in June, God's waiting room,
a nap at two, gin and tonic at five

Julie Maclean

Bunurong Eagle's Nest

Did people know it as Eagle's Nest
that name we call our coastal bay?
Did Bunurong people who lived
where silent land hosts the sea
where eagles today observe us,
also clamber over rocks like crabs?

Do the spirits of eagles watch there
beneath protected cliffs above,
where they saw you below
along the coast where you rested
tired after singing your own song,
listening to voices telling stories
on land where you knew
game emus and bush turkeys,
in places now silent beside the sea?

Did women gathering shellfish
keep distance, respect lairs
believing Banjil's protection
would order high seas to calm chaos,
silent flooding inundating coastal sites
long forgotten, where we meet again,
hopeful that we can dream as one?

Adèle Ogiér Jones

Turning Barrel

The barrel slowly turns
marbles roll and chatter
– until one escapes

number nine intones the grey suit
dates of birth solemnly written
posties deliver letters in many streets
official words chill family hearts
fit young men chosen by turn of the barrel
taken from desk and bench
bearing rifles on ships to Vietnam
SOS* mothers go to gaol
protesting youth burning draft cards
their brothers show courage under fire
and two hundred don't come home
objectors sitting in gaol cells
our country divided by turn of the barrel.

Geoff Graetz

* SOS: Save Our Sons

Country

Where is Country?
It is anywhere, and everywhere.
It is that portion of the curved globe
where you put your foot, and feel
there is something beneath
that supports, holds you up.
Without it you might sink
beneath the surface, and disappear.
It is where you might feel from the dirt
beneath your feet a bodiless tremor
that speaks silently to you. It is where
your skin touches the air, and light
falls like a cloak about you,
just you, and light, and air, and earth.
Where is Country? It is nowhere,
and timeless: it lives in your mind,
bored deep into your soul;
you have not seen it, you have not touched it,
you have not tasted it: the ghosts of your past
have lived it, they whom you have known
out of time and place: they join with you
in the great circling dance
of the breath of your life which is Country.

Robert Dickins

Advance Australia

Poised upon this palimpsest,
a debatable location
upholding a limitless sky.
The past, like ash, beneath my feet.

This cream, suburban home,
paint peeling inexorably
on an idly sloping hill.
Peeling back to a German vineyard
torn from the Yuggera
with force aplenty:
once a site of ceremony
and initiation,
guarded still
by Ancestor Spirits.

Feet mired;
minds otherwise wired
to oblivious technology,
obligingly taking our pills.

Our boots with constancy
scuffing across History,
buried meaningless inside
the vaults of an invisible past.

Raymond Evans

This is Jenn   & this is Eva   as one

from Watkin Tench: *a claim to land disputed*   *– Sydney Cove*
per Dorothy Hewett: *read more ways than one*   *– 'Sydney P.S.'*

It's all lighting up   this Geneva Convention   Centre
with our live cross   in essence affirmed   all thought
seen as auspicious   after fierce debate   with a focus
despite sharp eyes   giving razor-wire views   on rights
sparking blunt calls   that hold us to account   worldwide
about choices made   with centres for detention   onshore & off
…our national day   no cause for celebration   on reflection
no Treaty Day here   unlike Maori & pakeha   face to face
no Bastille stormed   if bleeding freely now free   in moving on
or July Fourth prized   with no pens making cuts   from a king
…dishonoured   as much in principle as   in reality
a day of invading   in fact: our first governor   stealing
unceded ground   giving lease to thieves   a prison
claimed in theft   with a Union Jack planted   in a cove…
spuds pinched later   inside his own fence   folk starving
canoes abandoned   beside the harbour no fish   nets empty
corpses on rocks   no answers to smallpox   thanks to us
a tribe even chased   with muskets & hatchets   such alarm
marines under orders   to avenge a gamekeeper   after a spear
impugned by name   stocking a guvnor's table…   in a turf war
first peoples dead   in cells kids stolen later   in white law
…at Geneva, Jenn   …Eva, on a big day   signing off…

Rodney Williams

history bites hard

history bites hard

leaving teeth-marks
to scar the hands
that feed it

so the gloves
of founding fathers
conceal a legacy

where strategic silence
is a handful
of red dust

through other hands

lost in statues
that brand faith
and historic asset

Adrian Flavell

Truths in Distant Times

Can we glimpse again those truths deep down,
the chips of memory left behind as time ran on,
those moments, keenly felt, but so often set aside
while teachers distributed their usual wisdom?

Can we find our way back to that peaceful bay
in evening light, where our dinghies lay upended
on the foreshore, arrayed beside the stalwart jetty,
as enterprising friends, like mariners of old,
brimful of quips and tales from past adventures,
stood armed with oars and nets and buckets,
ready to embark as lights across the bay came on?

What we learnt in other days often came by chance,
just this and that, enough to start each day afresh,
the ways at home, ways of opening up the world,
enchanting summers, school so far behind us then
it scarcely seemed to matter, as if the only truths
worth knowing were in our dinghies, or in the bay.

They will surely come to us again, when needed,
these lessons from beyond the classroom, drawn from
distant evenings, the deeper truths we usually obey.

Nicholas Hasluck

Such is Life

A response to Australia's first press photograph – Joe Byrne strung up outside the Benalla Gaol.

A grainy documentary,
fog-wrapped in white,
high whine of winter wind,
calcified hope.
Standing like a puppet in front of the lock-up,
his coiled weight pirouettes.
Long-legged Joe dances on tiptoes,
avoiding the chill of the ground below.
Dizzied and stiff-necked, arms angled,
eyebrows slightly raised,
his hand placed where his gun might be,
fine tuning his last move,
rehearsing the quick draw.

A paucity of light,
enough for the hooded photographer,
death always in a hurry
to make the print deadline.
Every event has lines leading back into the past,
into the future, into contrived famines
and forced migrations, into colonies, genocide,
into believable lies.

Anthony Mills

Ghost Gum

amongst eucalypts you are a cult figure
painted by Albert Namatjira
and anthologised in Aboriginal Dreaming
as the *Tree of Knowledge*

in 1891 before there were union halls
and street rallies
you were a gathering point
for striking shearers

seasonally you strip off
your pink bark corset
exposing your silvery skin
and wax-like texture

your branches are rented out
to a jukebox of native bird sounds
you are high-heeled and sun-hardened
and taller than a ship's mast

yet mostly you stay unnoticed
in your arid landscapes until nightfall
when against a blackboard sky
your trunk is chalked in

Jules Leigh Koch

from A Tasmanian Epic Poem

(Sonnet 57, Book 15)

'Not worth abo poo, is it cob?'
A fellow-viewer asked of me
At a mixed Nolan–Tucker show,
Saying further, 'at least the boongs
Have art that grows out of the land
They've lived in for millennia.
This WASP stuff's only fake from blokes
Who've lost their pommy heritage,
Belonging neither here nor there,
But huddling dispossessed along
The coast away from what's not theirs,
The vast desert interior
That's nearly all this country they'll
Never fathom as does a black!'

Graeme Hetherington

Pie-oneers

Australian Culture
is like a Pie Floater;
we didn't invent pies
or soup.

The pies do not float
and all of the pie carts
went out of business.

In all honesty,
no one asked for
what we claimed
to be ours.

Andrew Drake

Pantoum for Uluru: 25 October 2019

Inclement weather – the Rock was closed today
By 9 a.m. there was a queue – then it turned fair
Tourists walked past signs placed by the Aṉangu
This is a sacred site, we ask that you do not climb

By 9 a.m. there was a queue – then it turned fair
Tomorrow they take her chains away
This is a sacred site, we ask that you do not climb
Silver scars snake up her beautiful red flank

Tomorrow they take her chains away
That hurt to view, make you wince
Silver scars snake up her beautiful red flank
They say scars heal with time

Chain hurts to view, makes you wince
Awed by presence, I tremble at the foot of Uluru
They say scars heal with time
Some are incensed – *Mate, it's our right*

Awed by presence, I tremble at the foot of Uluru
Some are incensed – *Mate, it's our right*
We bin climbin' that rock for years, since the 60s
Aṉangu, bemused. *Mate, we bin here mebbe 50,000 years*

Sue Aldred

settler's debt

there's blood soaked into the soil
beneath my feet (covered in concrete)

there's blood on my hands
I cannot get it out, this blood on my hands

I cannot look away from the blood on my hands
from the blood on the soil (trampled by hooves)

from the smell of the blood
on this stolen soil (poisoned with pesticides)

I cannot get out the blood from the seven
generations of settlers who came before me

I cannot look away from my ancestors
farming land that was not theirs
planting seeds, growing livestock
building shelters that did not belong
on the land that was not theirs

land   *covered in concrete*
         trampled by hooves
         poisoned with pesticides
                  this land, hurting

Indrani Perera

Faded – *reflections no. 2*

so many reflections dust the pane
so many pages block the view
so many assumptions held as fact
so many reflections chase the mould –

there's fluttering at the windows,
the deadlines stacked the walls,
it's the oracle without license
it's the journalese that drowns the song:
they say *we don't learn from history,*
so who, is supposed to learn?

And the mean dust raked the pages, the headlines
rip the phrase, the faded print lost the date
there's no time to second-guess, and those lazy tags
cram the Flag as Gofers pass Conga like:
so, who's the reader? Who's the chief?
it's always been the same! And those flighty shoulders

can't find truths once passed as absolutes, distantly
we walk so close; it is inertia that carries the load.
And the dusty walls remain hidden, glass reflections
hang paper thin, now everybody holds a card:
it is the eternal muse! So *who* is supposed to learn?

David Taylor

Black Rights

blak rites
A long time coming.
A long time to understand.
A short time to get confused.
The human need for recognition is vitally important.
Who am I?
Who are you?
Who are those black people
living on the outskirts of life?
To answer one requires an answer to the many.
It will take a long time to get under our skin.

Antonia Reiseger

Time Capsule

Ancestors summoned in a poetic seance
           are bitter-lipped at our folly,
insistent we face our descendants.

Future generations we cannot know
           judge us for greed and intolerance,
           for sabotaging the environment.
They champion none of us as heroes.

Time travel is beyond us, but not beyond verse:
to talk to them, to apologise, to petition for empathy,
           we place this anthology in a time capsule.

Tell us, how do politics work
           in that future of yours,
           does democracy remain,
           are the monied even richer than here and now?

Tell us, did you untangle it all,
           with your creativity and restraint,
           your passion and logic, and a trace of AI?
Could you reverse what we caused?

Remorseful tears well up as I ask,
does 'Australia' still exist?

                                      Derek Baines

A metaphor for hope

In a time of loss and deep despair
        in a season of horrific world events

a tender stem of my mandevilla
        that held a single dark red flower

was severed nearly through.
        I bound it up with hope

it would not die.
        Now, even in a heat wave

the flower lives and on the stem
        another one is opening.

Pip Griffin

This Storied Land

The way he stood that night in his carport bent forward
under the engine hood of his rusty Ford was like an old
tracker looking down at the earth for the way to take.
Not that I knew anything then about this country, un-
familiar and isolating, ours the last two houses on a
road out into vast, grey timber, him with his pale, sun-
damaged face wheezing up stories out of stale lungs
like the rough churn of his engine, stories that went
all the way back to hard, long-distance crossings. Only
the moon is the same here, I thought. But would it do
me any good, mulling how to adapt and grow, under
a bare bulb burning out a piece of the dark, to listen
to all the dislocated histories, to the regress and
rescindment of old lives like mine marking us part of
this short catalogue of works? Then there were those
women I saw that other night, sat talking under an arc
of sky as if for millennia; like they were one with the
fixed constellations turning round them, or with the
moon voicing its own oratorio to the shared heavens;
like what matters is always having ground to mark
ourselves to. I'd be unanswerable to the story of here
unless I listened to every voice, to know how to reply;
to stories scattered like random collisions finding
new hold and belonging; or set sure, enduring like
the moon's that track all the way back to the stars.

Philip Radmall

Contest

At the turn of a tap, water fills my glass.
Images of our great south land, wrestling
many spectra of stewardship, flood in:
borders, wealth, empathy, greed.

This driest continent is not alone.
Our planet faces natural disasters, compounded
by human decisions that trail through history.
Media narrates stories into our lives.

Early explorers searched for a mythical sea
to explain the flow of the inland rivers; Trim
and his master missed the mouth of the Murray;
First Peoples shared waterholes – to their dismay.

Oceans and seas cradle our country, feed our
river systems and artesian basins. Bottled water
on our grocery shelves alerts us to the contest –
economic gain versus environmental survival!

Michael Keating

We Did Not Know Then

Ignorance is not meant as
some poor excuse for lethargy
that much admired Australian attitude
cheerfully trotted out as 'She'll be right mate'

The government who welcomed us as migrants
fifty years ago did nothing to make us aware
of Australia's real and very harsh history

So desperate were we for a new start
we did not know that our good fortune
was had at the expense of Aboriginal peoples
whose lands had been overtaken and plundered
whose lives and culture desecrated

Today we cannot say we did not know
we cannot plead ignorance
rather we are guilty of wilful disregard
showing the world how little self-respect we have
preferring to believe the voices of greed and follow
'She'll be right mate'
But for who is it right mate?

Brenda Eldridge

Straightness

Surveyors, standing on an eminence,
decreed a line to run
direct to the next.
Gums and sheoaks,
unmoved by the event,
swayed across the line.
Bandicoots and bilbies
ran beneath.
The worgalling of magpies
went every way.

The survey men stood
in a women's secret place.
Men of Country following a songline
stopped to gasp in horror.
Justice straight decreed
that spears be directed.

The barrels of surveyors' guns,
turned and bored,
now turned dead straight.

The survey line remained
invisible, impalpable, implacable.

John Lowe

The Keeper

'Who?'
White feet on red sand
'Who goes?'
Awake, we are
And feel the trespass

Spirits of the land
Ghosts in the rock
Watch with ancient eyes.
You are not alone in this land
Remember…

Jeannie Lawson

Sunday Drives

Childhood Sundays
With one hand steering the FJ Holden, Dad belted out
Johnny O'Keefe songs on the road to Sherbrooke Forest.
A lyrebird once fanned its tail and danced for me.
I wished and wished a koala,
Wedged in a tree fork, would wake and blink down at me.
Always disappointed. Except once!
Easter Sunday
Dad promised an ice cream on Phillip Island.
Little penguins lurched around my feet.
Forgotten ice cream dripped.
Summer Sunday
FJ windows wide open
On the heat-softened road to the Dandenongs.
Blurry shapes lay languid in the haze.
Would a kangaroo hop for me? 'Too hot,' Dad said.
Recent Sunday
Old woman silent on an intercity highway,
Windows closed for the air conditioning.
Kangaroo carcasses, wombat roadkill,
Blackened trees no home for birds.
The living creatures I had seen
Were they a childhood dream?
Were they a childhood dream?

Helen Lyne

Not One In a Hundred

You wake to the roar of helicopters, tracking to and
fro, over your roof. Fire? Cliff fall? Flash flooding?
An off-coast low shifts in and out, as clouds jettison
their cargoes. At dusk, lightning flickers, the horizon
an uneasy backdrop. Distant thunder drumming.

You grew up in the northern hemisphere, knowing
the rhythm of spring, summer, autumn, winter
as a trusted constancy in an unpredictable life.
On reaching Australia, you came to understand
how its vast landmass, has a multiplicity of seasons.

Yet in your chosen regions, those seasons had their own
predictability. You knew when to expect the jasmine
to bloom; which month was best for planting rocket;
when birds would return after autumn migration;
the right time to start stacking wood for winter.

One year of changes might be overlooked – as
'one in a hundred' perhaps, but now all blinkers
are ripped off. For survivors of floods and fires,
for farmers who work the land, for the many
who despair as our natural world loses ever more
native species – there is no salvation in denial.

Gillian Telford

In Whose Name?

> the shadow-side
> of a flapping flag…
> a nation
> or misfits seeking identity
> in a stolen land?

on the menu
at the War Memorial café
digger's breakfast
they're serving wilted spinach
in the trenches now

> in brass
> on the remembrance wall
> so many names
> written in blood
> on a foreign shore

in the rubble
of everyday lives
upturned
kitchen chair, cooking pot
child's teddy bear

> again, the present
> tosses history aside…
> in whose name
> do we create
> the evening news?
>
> *Michelle Brock*

Blood Orange Crown

after an artwork by Sue Kneebone, *The Sunken Garden…*

I am an intricate crown of woven seaweed,
once caressed and teased by tides and waves,
my fine locks moving in water's breeze,
myriad fish combing and curling my fringe.
My tendrils grew longer and longer –
Rapunzel's plait, inviting sea life to climb up
and kiss my soft damp skin.
My garden fed the visiting hoards
as I drank in sun and grew towards a god light.
I danced to the beat of the moon
her magnetic pull turned my feet
her magical rhythms waltzed me,
to and fro, in a full-moon ballroom.

But it is the era of oil spills and engines,
of floating factories robbing my home,
of men with nets, harpoons, and fish prisons.
It is the era of rogue plastic, ghost nets,
choking, torturing and maiming.
And now, I am a circular symbol
of man's stranglehold beneath the surface.
Bless the artist who gave me voice,
who wove me into a crown of thorns,
a wreath to prickle human conscience.

Jude Aquilina

Glamping

A tour across the Great Sandy Desert
along the historic Canning Stock Route
offers the luxury of Mercedes Benz
with travelling shower and toilet block.
Camps are set up to be comfortably plush
and gourmet meals are served with finest wines.
The glossy brochure speaks of native art.
It doesn't mention massacres and neck chains.

When this route was first surveyed
natives were kept in chains and force-fed salt,
released when driven mad with thirst
and followed to their sacred water-holes.
The wells established for the stockmen's use
could not be accessed by the desert people.
Now tourists think of water as the source
of ice for their evening gin and tonic.

Outside the circle of the camp-fire's glow
sad shadowy figures gather in the dark
waiting to tell their stories to the world.

Mary Jones

Pool of Tears

Reconciliation Park, Karinya Reserve, Eden Hills SA

Water tumbles over Aboriginal faces
carved in bold ancient rock.

Near a circle of gum saplings,
and the fountain's rustic reeds,

a sculptured mother sits bereft,
arms empty in an ache of sorrow.

Shards of sunlight shatter like glass.
Water trickles like infinite tears.

Overhead, a clamour of cockatoos
lifts into blue skies.

All around, light bounces and shifts
like skinks darting through grasses.

In this place of peace and beauty,
Nature soothes, honours and heals.

Jayne Linke

2 p.m. Sunday, 6 July 1835

*A giant of a man, European in appearance but in a
native's garb, shambled into the camp left by John
Batman at Indented Head, near Geelong.*

Why did I run off with the other convicts?
For freedom, of course! But nothing was possible
until I met the Aboriginals.
Saw the way they greased themselves and danced;
heard their stories and inner music. They showed me
the land's plants and creatures; weather and seasons.
Nothing could exceed their kindness – though they
constantly warred with other tribes over territory,
women and provisions. I rejected their cannibalism,
becoming their equal as a hunter and provider.
I continued to pray to my God, though I lost the
use of English and my sense of time.
The natives believe white men are just
their dead brothers – returned to earth after death.

*The man did not speak a recognisable word,
until he was offered a slice of bread. The colony had
not seen him for 32 years. He was William Buckley.*

Danny Gardner

Material in italics sourced from *Life and Adventures of William Buckley*

Australian Horizon

after all we've been through –
the flood waters haven't subsided
the fires can never be extinguished
& the Virus is always among us
& Indigenous voices were silenced
& refugees are still being imprisoned
& the trickle-down effect has stalled
at the top floor while the homeless
sleep on the street   existentially
we've been hurled into the Antipodes
condemned to be authentic & free
(hopefully without a a future
filled with AI deep fakes)   &
even the Queen must die   hard to
believe she failed to dodge
that bullet but it all ended
with uplifting voices & a longing
for everlasting solace   all we
can wish for is that fairness &
kindness become the default
positions & the best bits from
the compassionate narratives
are delivered with regularity to
everyone's inbox

Carolyn Gerrish

Threshold

31 December 2023

In a month of heat and thunderstorms we've retreated to this weary weatherboard dwelling, furnished with discarded hopes and sagging armchairs, op-shop china and bargain-table finds. I try on a forgotten blue shirt, stained and faded like the summer sky: it no longer fits. I ignore the sandy floor, cobwebby shells on the windowsill, tufts of dog hair floating down the hall on the gentle sea breeze. We escape out back, screen door slapping after us, the dog just managing to slip through. Ten paces, no fences, and we are on the bush track – banksia leaves, brown and crisp like Christmas baking, crunch beneath our boots. We slap mozzies, dodge bull ants, are wary of each branch on the sandy earth. Worimi children, naked and unshod, surely ran this path chasing a goanna – how did they know how to avoid the bull ant, mosquito, the snake bite? Our year, like a film of opaque paper laid over a map, records months that hardly at all match the blossoming of boronia, the sway of Christmas bells, the taste of the changing wind, the bright flowering field of flannel stars

> *perhaps*
> *the way things have always*
> *been done*
> *is not the only way*
> *we can be*

Julie Thorndyke

First Farms

At the start the convict colony grew hungry
for fertile farming land.
Sydney soils proved ungenerous
so the year after the First Fleet
Governor Phillip sailed the Hawkesbury River
finding fertile upper river flats
a bread basket for the colony.

Farming started with a land grant
to an emancipated convict at Green Hills.
War raged for decades with Darug First People
before a treaty took their land.
Governor Macquarie named the growing region Windsor.
Later the gold rush brought red brick buildings.

Now crops dot the nation to feed and export
while past Sydney's urban rim of light industry
past new developments with high density housing
a thin band of eucalypts, wattle and casuarinas
borders the preserved town of Windsor
an early step in a history of loss.

Paul Williamson

In the Glare

Fragum erugatum

On the turquoise-blessed west coast
there's a sandless beach for the crunch
under feet; for the sieve of childlike hands:

cockles forming the ridges of the foreshore.
We're standing among trillions of them on
Shell Beach, each small as a young thumb.

They spread for kilometres I'm told, metres
deep in places. Once alive in the hyper-saline
water, solar-powered and buffered by algae.

And nearby, past the shell quarry of soft-stone
coquina, there's a telegraph station crammed
with memorabilia in grey and black, from 1884.

We step outside to the molluscs of the dunes
gathered after thousands of years of storm-
and wave-surge; they lie dazzling in the glare.

Kathryn Fry

For a Young Australian

When our prayers go up, they fly as broken glossolalia
bent in flight as arrows sprung from compound bows
might rim the sky to circumnavigate a rough horizon,
landing with a thud to penetrate the fletcher's heart,
who trimmed a feather close to boomerang the path.

When our braying tones crack the glass through which
the hypervigilant sentries of the gods spy, the shatter
splinters deep into the Other's eye, with a shudder felt
from Darwin to Woomera, at Nhulunbuy where rockets
launch satellites whose gaze defies protective shields.

I pray that you may ride under the radar of the drones,
through the bardo states of Facebook and white Twitter,
and not be seduced by the soaring real estate market
of Sydney. Learn humility, act justly, love tenderly.
Find courage to stay when I have passed into the light.

These convoluted songlines of my prayer for you come
plucked as feathers from a condemned duck's wet back.
Soft as down, they take to the winds, riding updrafts
into the dreaming of what always was, flying as geese
in their last Kakadu days, before the wetlands drown.

Andrew Leggett

Dear River Authorities

Further to the recent large-scale fish death event, we request an immediate review of the oxygen levels in the Murray-Darling Basin.

We acknowledge their depletion is due to warmer weather and wonder if you would be so kind as to re-evaluate your environmental priorities to mitigate further increases in atmospheric temperature?

We, in turn, will try our utmost to breathe a little less and wherever possible, refrain from extensive periods of swimming.

Your prompt consideration of this matter would be greatly appreciated.

Yours sincerely

The Surviving Relatives of those who Perished

J V Birch

Plaited History

Ribbons of ancient history
slip through our fingers,
trailing impressions and records
beyond our knowledge
into the present then –
slipping their moorings
and moving on and on and on.
Murmurings of 'in my day'
or 'things used to be'
belie a sense of mistrust,
yet wonder too as
new born ideas pop
like hot corn,
scorching the too eager,
baffling the cautious.
The past is swallowed,
regurgitated, swallowed again
as futures in our land
spew out changes too quickly
too new,
too incalculable,
too wondrous to absorb.

Margo Poirier

Four Generations

You were my gentle grandad
I was spoilt and loved, the first female of your line
Quietly spoken grower of delicate gladioli
You named one after me
Companioned by your loyal springer spaniel
But never told me about Fromelles
The horror of your war
Just grew the sweetest strawberries.
You were my upright father
Brilliant but Depression deprived
Lived for service and duty
Pressured night study late in life broke your health
I think you loved me.
I am still living and loved; married
Have played, planted and bought houses
Studied, travelled, written books and made music
Flourished in my female way
Gathered my grandchildren around me
Some say I am a lucky boomer.
Dear granddaughter, finished school, finding your way
Tossing the dark curls bestowed by my genes
Driving a car to university
Free to choose your life or even gender
Inheriting a broken beautiful world I leave to you
With love and some sorrow.

Jeanette Woods

Fearful

Putting up fences, hoping for safety
No more risking unknowns
Fencing off past mistakes and shapeless fears
Controlling our future as best we can
Frightened of strange hands that reach for help
Carefully choosing who gets close
Only family and a few like us

Maybe the Mafia got it right

David Meldrum

After the Referendum 2023

Here you are

turning away from despair

The banksia too
holds life and seed inside a thick case
made from its own self and from the earth

After fire it births a form
both different and the same

Warning:
If fire after fire occurs
with no between time
for the spirit box to refill…

Helen Swain

www.ingramcontent.com/pod-product-compliance
Lightning Source LLC
Chambersburg PA
CBHW070951080526
44587CB00015B/2256